NOT IN THESE SHOES

Samantha Wynne-Rhydderch was born in west Wales, where she still lives.

D0313845

Also by Samantha Wynne-Rhydderch

Rockclimbing in Silk

NOT IN
THESE SHOES

Samantha Wynne-Rhydderch

PICADOR

First published 2008 by Picador
an imprint of Pan Macmillan Ltd
Pan Macmillan, 20 New Wharf Road, London N1 9RR
Basingstoke and Oxford
Associated companies throughout the world
www.panmacmillan.com

ISBN 978-0-330-45146-8

Copyright © Samantha Wynne-Rhydderch 2008

The right of Samantha Wynne-Rhydderch to be identified as the
author of this work has been asserted by her in accordance
with the Copyright, Designs and Patents Act 1988.

All rights reserved. No part of this publication may be
reproduced, stored in or introduced into a retrieval system, or
transmitted, in any form, or by any means (electronic, mechanical,
photocopying, recording or otherwise) without the prior written
permission of the publisher. Any person who does any unauthorized
act in relation to this publication may be liable to criminal
prosecution and civil claims for damages.

9 8 7 6 5 4 3 2 1

A CIP catalogue record for this book is available from
the British Library.

Printed and bound in the UK by
CPI Mackays, Chatham ME5 8TD

This book is sold subject to the condition that it shall not,
by way of trade or otherwise, be lent, re-sold, hired out,
or otherwise circulated without the publisher's prior consent
in any form of binding or cover other than that in which
it is published and without a similar condition including this
condition being imposed on the subsequent purchaser.

ESSEX COUNTY
COUNCIL LIBRARY

Visit www.picador.com to read more about all our books
and to buy them. You will also find features, author interviews and
news of any author events, and you can sign up for e-newsletters
so that you're always first to hear about our new releases.

For Cosmo, Bob, Brychan and Cristyn and to the memory of Kirsty MacColl (1959–2000)

Thanks are due to the editors of the following journals in which some of these poems first appeared: *New Welsh Review*, *Planet*, *Poetry London* and *Poetry Wales*. 'Rowndio'r Horn' was commissioned by BBC Wales for National Poetry Day 2001 and first appeared in the anthology *The Pterodactyl's Wing*, ed. R. Gwyn (Parthian, 2003).

I would like to thank both Yr Academi Gymreig and The Society of Authors for awarding me a bursary to enable me to write this collection. I am grateful to the Hawthornden Foundation for a fellowship in 2005, to my sister, Francesca, and to the staff at the Brontë Parsonage Museum. The manuscript has benefited greatly from the critical eye of my editor, Don Paterson, and from the support and encouragement of Kate Clanchy, Colette Bryce, Henry Shukman and Nathalie Wourm. Finally I would like to thank Henry and Margaret Parry for an attic to write in.

Contents

Découpage

The day of your post mortem
I cleaned the kitchen
to blot out the hour you'd be cut up,

made apple pie, scrubbed the table
again, wondering how
you were getting on. If you were here

you'd be sat there with your pinking shears
thinking in appliqué, stencilling
quilted queens: Branwen, Marie-Antoinette,

long-necked with their net coronets,
sewn into chiffon gowns, sequins pinned into their eyes,
silk lips slit into diamonds, their cheekbones

slashed indigo lines.
I reconstruct your mosaic face
in my head as I wash up, I,

restricted by nine stitches in my back,
itself a collage of red lines and thread,
my deckle-edged tumour out of the picture now.

We were trying to piece you together,
your new tenant explains on the phone,
what you leave behind tells a story, doesn't it?

Backless

I'll take it. And that was how
I bought my second skin, my dress
with half the back scooped out.

Swathed in fish-scale, I teetered
along the shop floor,
in sequins, tall with a train. My tail

late in my wake, I swished down
the hall. On a gondola I slid,
raw, silked, my back silvery,

an opaque window of skin.
At two a.m., an inverted arch:
my dress, peeled off and slung

over an arm that was not yours
but the croupier's, his back
foursquare to me, mine shimmering

like the sweep of the bay
under the stars. Later, the wardrobe
door let it all hang out, his life

in all its hues: racing green, duck white,
Maxwell blue. *Maxwell*, name of a sloop
whose mast stood fast in the floor

of our house, a backbone
stripped of her assets, like me
in my set-piece dress. Spineless?

Listen, I'm a roulette babe, able
to put my own spin on any white
tie-and-tails. When he appeared

backlit in the marquee, gathering
his pieces of eight, intoning his odds
in the small hours, my bets were long

placed, half-size maple-backed violin
that I was against the wall,
enthralled by his lapels, trailing

my signature river down the stone
staircase towards the swoop of his wing,
his tails arranged like a decision to live.

The Stain

Come to think of it, in a certain light
it looked ochre, all down the staircase,
marking the site of some terrible accident,

except that we all knew it had been tea
and that it was me who had dropped the tray,
collecting every fragment before an audience

of twenty in the hotel lobby, going to pieces
but acting like it was a regular clear-up.
The interior scar I lived with for months

like your death at twenty-one. Six weeks
before you jumped, you gave me your old desk –
but it was only after you'd leapt that I found

the inkstain in one of the rosewood drawers
and thought about the colour of the stones on the shore.

Wheelbarrow

The ivy's writing along
a redbrick wall

reminds me of the scrawl
of the sight test,

aged six, when asked to
identify a picture of a small

container with one wheel
and two legs. *Whîlber*

was the only word
I had for that,

so I pretended it was my sight
that was at fault.

My vision now is clearer
as I guide the barrow up

the steep paths of the orchard.
Outlines of caravans are etched

in rows on gardens sold
by court order in the fifties

so people could have a holiday
with a view. Now I have a view

of them all year round.
There's a word for that

in my third language, only
it's slipped my mind.

71,200 *Megalitres*

The twelfth of August nineteen sixty-five:
the day my mother cried,
taken as a child to file
through Capel Celyn valley,

protesting, one final time. Four days on,
the flooding would begin.
The sun poured down, anglophone
onto six rows of onions

in the garden of Bryn Ifan. Upstairs
Beti Cae Fadog trimmed
geraniums, unable
to pack. The day following

was the day when the family dresser
would be emptied, upturned,
roped flat like a makeshift raft.
The Drowning then began

at dawn on the sixteenth, the two-hundred-
year old elms round the farm
cut down, piled up like bodies,
burnt. Compulsory purchase

order – the whole story was not quite known
until now: livelihoods
had just been stolen from them
in code. Try to drain away,

if you can, from your head, the opaque face
of the lake, complicit
curator of drowned traces
of hearths and rooms; think of

evictions, of watching your home engulfed.
A film on the net lasts
ten seconds of silence where
a postman stumbles up to

the neat gate of Ty'n y Rhos. A caption
says *an old man opens*
his front door for the last time.
Only the curtains were left,

his furniture shouldered the day before
like empty coffins and
the trellis demolished. Still
the writing on the walls calls:

Cofiwch Dryweryn. In these rare moments
of drought, our whole farmhouse
can be seen again. Hundreds
come from miles to count the steps

to the back door, harder to endure than
a lake full of itself.
On the day mum was led to
say goodbye to the submerged

dead forever, she saw the last tulips
she'd laid on her young aunt's
grave eight days before, crimson
as mouths across the surface.

Crayfish Tail Salsa

Hotel Reception

8 stone 2.
There's only so far you can go
on an island a mile long.
That was just on Wednesdays,
my day off. On the other six
I'd spend eight hours a day in a
cupboard. True, every office has one
you can escape to. There,
it *was* the office,
a sixteenth-century one at that.
I'd hear reports, of course,
from the world outside the castle walls.
What did I see of it? Sixty seconds
of sunset when I'd run outside
to change the daily menus,
a new version of the same poem.

Kitchen

8 stone.
On a good day and if he hadn't had
that extra pint at lunchtime,
the head chef, Jim, would only
scream at me twice to f– off

when I'd go in at five to get
the menu checked. Ravenous
as I was, there was no place
I'd rather not be than hear the reply to
Any changes to the menu, Jim?
Crayfish Tail Salsa was one
his glass eye would miss,
that little dance in sauce tripping
off the page. The closest I came
all year to writing poems was
deciding where the line breaks would go
in the menus Jim would spit out.
By the way what's the difference
between 'a tossed salad' and 'a salad'?
Isn't all salad tossed? By a tosser?

Hunger

7 stone 12.
Working in a hotel? F**r St*r food every day!
Chips mainly. *Look at this*
one of the kitchen girls hissed
opening a fist to reveal the dull eye
of a fish. Any good at problem solving?
If staff tea is at 5 every day
and you are on duty 2 till 10pm
six days with no breaks,
how do you eat? Leave your desk
for one minute, whisk out a side plate
containing four mouthfuls

of cold mushroom risotto. Feast
on the dishes of the menu as you
type them out. Read the checks
slowly: 2 x camembert,
2 x pheasant, 1 x mousse.
At 10 I'd be allowed to
pick fruit out of the bin
whilst a waiter soothed the floor
with water, shoulderblade to the wall,
Woody Guthrie throating out cotton field lyric
long forty years ago.

Anger

7 stone 3.
A juggler of irons and phones, cream teas
and keys. Not that he'd see it that way,
your boss. The best way to run a hotel is
to get one person to do three jobs. PS. It's you.
Why not write a one-act play
in your head while answering two phones?
Scene 1 is where you're limping
with an iron and board to room 42,
sprinting back in Manolos
to make tea for six in the library
whilst a colonel is waiting
to be shown to the conservatory.
In Scene 2 you're already
answering line 1 when line 2 rings.
Why don't you answer the phone!

There's a lady at the poolside
who wants fresh towels! With jam?
It would be funny if it wasn't
happening to me, six days a week
for a year. I didn't bother writing Scene 3.

Dungeon

7 stone.
After dinner, they'd all repair to the Dungeon Bar,
the guests, the chefs and the chambermaids,
freshly pressed after Turndown.
It would be as if the rooms had been visited by a
fairy who riffled through the linen and folded open
the first page of the Book of Bed.
Sleep on this, the sheets seemed to speak,
these beds of weddings: the low-key,
the high-powered, the third time around.
Occasionally I'd drink there too, in the bar,
celebrating the arrivals and departures
of those who'd been to a cinema only two nights before.

Leaving the Island

6 stone 13.
Flowers. That's what kept you going all year,
wasn't it? A bunch of sweet peas
I'd buy for a pound once a week,
their smell so delicious I could've
eaten them. Except by then I'd lost
my appetite. Three days to go, said
the calendar. I was too weak to
carry my case down to the quay,
so they drove me those a hundred yards
in a boneshaker Land-Rover.
Every flight and ferry cancelled by storms,
there was only one way out.
I caught the freight ship back
to England in a thirty-five-knot wind.
So that was me and four crewmen for five hours
in heavy seas. I queased
on deck watching it all recede:
the parapets, the gardens, the boathouse,
the agapanthas, Watermill Cove where
something had eluded me at the water's edge
in the sharp light of autumn, birdcall purpling
away. When I could fit it all into
the palm of my hand, I held my hunger
there like the one pebble I brought back
as a souvenir. At the dockside
in Penzance I floated off the ship and did a
little jig. *What's that?* they said. *Crayfish*

Tail Salsa, that little dance in sauce I never got
to taste, I said and headed off to
the poshest restaurant in town.

Oyster Forks

1000.
Asparagus tongs: 400
Dinner plates: 12,000
Champagne glasses: 1,500
Eggs: 40,000
Sausages: 35,000
Flower Vases: 500
Sheets: 18,000
Rivets: 3,000,000
Marconi Wireless Operators: 2
Crew: 891
Passengers: 1,317
Lifeboats: 20

Titanic

Cadences
before water filled the open lung
of the baby grand.

Conversation

A fork down the throat
of the loo left me speechless
in the interval.

Give Me Another Word For It

You knock at my door with your violin unstrung.
I ask you in. You ask me to stand before a watercolour

with you, as if this simple act could dilute
your guilt, create a stunt double you might send home

to your wife in the bedroom, where two pylons loom,
dissect the view, their hum your constant song,

out of tune. Electricity. That's what I hear
in my veins. I want to write it out. Your words

interrupt the lines in my head, bisecting a life
of art. Have them back, your voice, the poems

which do not rhyme, the lines you forgot, couplets
you never quite found an ending for. See this,

in a jar, on the shelf, in the corner
of the cupboard, unlabelled? It's called

diamonds and rust, the cremation
of a decade. You can keep it. Or shall I stir it

into this cup of tea you asked me for?
Then you can taste it all: me ground down,

sitting by the phone, dusted with tragedy ...
Not likely. Ten years ago you stayed at home

weaving your stagnant tale whilst I travelled the world
with my pen eloping from island to island. Guess

the colour of this kiss you try to poach from me now,
all the lies unwritten at your feet, whilst I, accurate

as the clock, move my hands in time to the verses you
have untapped from my tongue by this one act of arrival

and departure. Take that word you can't articulate
away with you. I'll keep the rest. I paid for them.

A Pair of Antlers

Ride a horse along the trail.
Glimpse
through leaves every tone of rust
and the jackdaws' call,
the towers of Ingledene,
intricate in the cliff,
my hair the colour of sandstone
on your collar,
only the voice of a decanter
and a northerly in the glen:
a language called Bliss.

The white hart caught again and again
on your wallpaper –
at night I'd hear it once more
from your turret bedroom,
a pair of antlers on the wall
adorned with your hat,
your shirt exhausted
on a tartan chair after a day at the axe.

High up in the south wing
I couldn't take my eyes off you
as you fought roots of rhododendrons,
the precipice below,
slow claimer of all our possessions
through a wide-open sash:
six of my books had already
blanched in the textured Esk.

You'd stand with a single malt,
in braces, admiring a Grinling,
while I did a fingertip search of your face,
woodsmoke and heather in the grate,
after leading me all day along the river
in spate, unintentional dancers,
discovering the recesses of baronial you,
lairding it in a rented estate
we were about to lose. So many rooms,
rooms of rooms. I would surprise myself
at dusk in gilded mirrors, disappear
behind an aspidistra the size of a small tree,
the ceilings ornate as my inarticulate heart.

At first just flakes, but as the months
wore on, more plaster started to fall.
Each evening as we read by the fire's soliloquy,
our chairs strident on the flagstones,
another piece of eighteenth-century horsehair
and lath would sigh onto the floor.
More Madeira, me dear? and you'd pour.

We'd pretend it wasn't happening, this falling apart:
was *decadence* really bordering on *decay*?
I held the drawing pins and you took white sheets.
We blanked it all out
with interior sails.

The Four Seasons:
An Exhibition of Chinese Painting

What are they saying
those two walking in whispers
up to an ancient

temple through water-
falls in the Ashmolean?
Beneath wisteria

a man plays a qin,
brushstrokes of a bird on a
flowering branch, thin,

a hint of shades from
the Southern Song dynasty.
A pale pine tree breathes

snow on streams. The Li
River on woodblock, with plum
blossom falling on

hibiscus and ducks,
like the confetti I bought
for Jo's wedding feast

and flung up into
the air, alone, as a jet
plane passed. You'd just left

to live in Beijing,
announced it one May under
apple leaves over

the Thames. There you go.
You never can tell how it'll
all not work out. I

leave the seasons turn.
Outside in St Giles, the trees
shake off autumn, burn.

Private View

Tails you lose, so for the exhibition
I fired ten ceramics as the apology
you never got round to making
in pen and ink. This one's a bijou collage

of all the phoneboxes I cried in as a waitress
between split shifts. That one's my glass slipper.
You see, it fits perfectly. Manolos, if you must
know. And here's a game of poker

made from the buttons of a shirt you left
behind, twisted and stuck on green felt.
Let me get this right, you both being lawyers,
did you say you were the loser and she the liar

or vice versa? Word for word, please.
Oh, and, can I have that in writing?

Under the Hammer

Whether Dora kept that lock of hair so
she could be buried with it wasn't clear
to us reading its calligraphic curl,
Lot 19, that she'd run her fingers through
on long evenings at Ménerbes, garnering
even then souvenirs of obsession.

His pebble portraits; bottletop birds; scraps
of paper bearing his bloodstains; her pink
gloves that wilted in her hands when he'd held
her mouth so close he couldn't read in its flower
the sorrow she knew she risked, its sculptor –
all this spread out here, under the hammer.

Matador

Stripped to the waist in a hotel room in Arles,
the sword-valet has already unbuttoned
the top three of the matador's mother-of-pearl
clasps when I, the cameraman, am ushered
in with the drapes half-shut against the molten
pavements, the faint baying of the crowd's desire
to see once more the blood-spattered ornate vine-
leaves woven in gold all the way up his thighs.

Cocksure in his cape he'd strutted beaded and clean
into the ring, prim in a waistcoat, on fire
for the bull as I was for him, my lens trained
on his torso, tasselled to the hilt. His arms'
geometry provoked the horns to a goring.
Then raised on the shoulders, an ear in each hand.

Brighton West Pier

Last week I saw it again, staggering
like a shot beast in the high tide,
the pavilion a skull half sunk, gnawing

at its stilts. A telephone receiver swung
from the tangled guts of the bar.
Of course I have witnessed dereliction before:

mantelpieces three floors up,
the remnants of passion fluttering
in the torn wallpaper of virtual rooms,

the cross-section of intimacy.
But this reclaiming by sea of our
tentative steps leaves me

precarious: those Saturday nights
when I would catch my breath outside
its stuccoed façade, stilettoed,

tiptoeing between strips of sea foaming
below, a note from a saxophone
thrown to the wind, hearing his voice

on the line half a century ago,

still swaying there.

Shaved

Take this one, for instance, from her own album:
Crown Duchess Tatiana, rollerblading, flirts
across the deck of the royal yacht, *Standart*;

or even in this one whilst under house arrest:
Anastasia, planting cabbage seeds and cress
is radiant in muslin, surrounded by guards.

May 4th, 1917: all five over
the mumps now, so my darlings had their heads shaved,
then were photographed in a line all in black!

The Execution Archive for that year states
the bald facts: at twelve the Romanovs were told
to dress, stand in a row. It was necessary

to finish off the girls with bayonets; their corsets,
laced with diamonds, had turned the bullets back.

Scribblemania

These tatty balloon-back
chairs, the large oak table
on flagstone floors

felt all too chilly
and familiar to be
on display. This

writing life
wasn't one I expected
to be roped off from

at seven when we
already lived it at home,
my sisters and I.

Handed a laminated
breadboard in the museum,
you'd have the whole story

on one side: of how they sat
and where and who was
the *real* Jane Eyre;

of the beadery and
composition of their three
dresses which took

turns for a place
by the fire, like us.
Even back then, I wasn't

one for the vapours
nor given to abridged versions
of already brief lives, nor

to those who wondered
aloud how the girls wrote
without central heating.

By layering, I thought, *like
a narrative,* as we paced
the boards like extras

auditioning for the role
of tenant in a wild hall
full of would-be writers,

80,000 of us a year
scrutinizing Charlotte's
shoes, willing them to

yield up the secret of
how to plot. Did she
wear these pumps for

promenades around
the table with her sisters,
pulling each sentence

apart every night? Years later
at MFI, my sisters and I are
taking stock of tables and chairs,

walking around new beds,
lingering in sliced rooms,
tracing roses on mattresses

that will always remain
unseen, woven yellow
beneath our dreams.

We talk of how a novel
will take you by the throat
at three a.m. and then

you understand *his* tone of voice
or why *she* crossed the lawn
at dusk and took his hand.

The thing about rope is
one usually ends up
the wrong side of it.

It's all in the chairs,
if you ask me. Threadbare
as the moors, what's left

of the horsehair where
the Reverend sat
is all we need to know.

The Naming Of The Storm

Anna-Louise

I awoke to find half an arm pinned
behind my back, my hair gone stiff.
Last thing I remembered was
him leaning over me, about to
carve out my right breast.
He left me speechless, with parted lips,
which he kissed and mounted me
on the head of this, his ship.
Anna-Louise! he yelled
and threw a bottle of Moët,
just missing my tits.
No, I wouldn't have called it a great
send-off either.

Shipwreck

They were on their third bottle of Courvoisier
when we hit the Gilstone at 49°, 55N.
I saw it coming, of course. Would do,
with the best view. Down below, the decanters
shivered as the wind got up,
night falling like a stage curtain.
In the teeth of a gale I was pitched up,
all hands on deck fighting the sails.

Too late. For most of us, the last thing we saw was
the rock that had stopped us in our track.
I spent the next two hundred years
on the seabed. Alone, may I add. And face down,
which explains why I'm so well-preserved.

You've Pulled!

Life is never the same once you are off the prow.
A diver took me in his arms
and that was it. I saw the light of day.
He made a few measurements, looked into
my eyes, had me valued. All night
I lay propped, insomniac,
my one good arm broken
at my side, holding a tiny flower
I once offered motionless to high seas,
day in day out. One-night stand.
He carted me off to a wreck-sale in Penzance.
The one who wrote the cheque
had spent six hours giving me the eye.
He decided I needed touching up.

The Figurehead Museum

There are about thirty of us in one room, all
nailed to pillars. We can't look each other
in the eye. At first we were exhibited
in the state the sea had given us up.

Now we are gaudy red and gold,
surprising members of the public
with our brash finery and fixed grins.
Through an open window I can hear the tide,
the voice of a stranger, the wind, my past.
Come in, I say, *I'll give you
shelter from the storm.*

Rowndio'r Horn

One by one they clipped the edge of the table
and smashed in the Lower Mess Deck, sixteen plates,
castanets. Whatever the candelabra, the sea
has reasons of its own. In the third watch she,
the mainsail, full-blown ivory, eighty-four
degrees to the wind, visceral to starboard
tore. Know her to be your shroud, think majestic
stone pier, tomb far from here, hers your cambric shirt.

Like everyone else in the Yacht Club, I pose
and tilt at Mar del Plata a hundred years
later, mermaid for the day, piña colada
in hand. Taffeta angle, sweet sail, did you
call out to me, at the helm, as my feet flew?

'Going round the Horn'. Many New Quay sea captains sailed round
Cape Horn and returned to tell the tale including my great-great-grand-
father, Captain Edward Jones ('Tadcu Stryd Ganol'), until his ship, *The
Adventurer*, was lost with all hands (including his nineteen-year-old
nephew) on a voyage from Taltal to Talcahuano off the coast of South
America in March 1893.

Abandonata

Above the stove his longjohns hang
where he pegged them on June 10th 1911.

A pin-up of a girl's naked back
beside his bunk is curling up to his

spilt shelf of charts and logs, the diary's yard
of ink. Frozen to death, outside,

the remains of a dog, chained in ice.
And here, Ponting's darkroom, reliquary

of vials and plates splayed like cards.
On the table where Scott raised a final

birthday glass, a visitor has tried a slice
of a hundred-year-old ham. Tins

of boiled mutton, brawn, Tate & Lyle
syrup lie thick and slow as the snow's

drift, preserving an era's hour.
And what of the women they left behind,

pausing each night on the stairs
to wind the heart of a clock,

folding and unfolding clothes, reading
and re-reading letters, weighing

each word, like a body?

Stately Home

The one thing I can recall is
the painted Swedish chair in the playroom,
a heart cut out of its back.
Which is how I feel now
as paint flakes off the gate.

There, on the hall table, would be
my mother's sequined gloves
in love with each other in a pool of light,
the faded purple curtains, the sanity
of doilies. Upstairs, my baby dresses

might lie like pressed flowers
under glass, unvisited,
my five-year-old voice trapped
in the cupboard in which I once
whispered a poem.

Round the back you'd see the sundial
pointing up to the Sychnant Mountain
I longed to climb, when every bedtime
I'd check my piece of driftwood,
still safe under the pillow.

The Sea Painter's House

The fox's teeth gleam in the firelight
as he walks rigid in his display case
hung over the spinet I have never heard
played. Only the music of the sea
moans across the verandah, locked out
in winter, its rough tongue whitening
the chairs. In the porch Miranda leans

to embrace every stranger, hands tied
behind her back, my father's figurehead.
She will lean that way forever,
earrings to match her low-cut dress,
nocturnal under streetlamps.
Yes, she wants you
as you limber back up the hill from
Tafarn y Roc, watching you all the way,
blue eyes flaking after six decades
on the prow. She is the keeper of
the furled-up oils, chrysalises
stowed in your studio between sextant

and sea-chest: too many ships to hang on the walls.
I know their names like old lovers: *The Blue Jacket*,
The Deb, The Friendship. Their still sails uncurl
in my sleep and sometimes we are both
at the helm of each vessel, my father and I,

he one side of the wheel and I the other, or carefully
he is tying knots on the aft deck whilst I,
aerial in the rigging, untwist his red ensign.
In our attic, the uniforms of all my dead
captains moth away, a tiny brass anchor
stamped on each button.

In The Bath

She was eighty-three
and had to die somewhere,
but what a place to spend
the weekend. *Just going for
a long soak*, she'd sung
down the phone. By nine
on Monday her voice
had overflowed through floorboards
and cupboards until it seeped through
the front door. *Romaine, Romaine!*
we called, forced a dripping window
and turned the hot tap
off. When we pulled the plug out
she was the same colour as
the Radox Aqua bath foam next to her head,
as if ready for burial on the seabed.

Ar Werth – For Sale

Grandfather Clock

For once I wasn't in love with the auctioneer.
I put my hand into your side, long and polished,
felt your entrails sleek through my fingers
like an anchor, your deep-throated tick
that stopped the day my grandpa died.
Your face was worn out, the inscription eroded
below the holy-eyed lion, the anvil lavishly
black. I raised a glass to you, tick tock,
the day you were carried off.

Reclamation

At least part of her garden is still there
even if the sea has reclaimed
the orchard. Just the tamarisk tree
shakes its head in a north-easterly
next to the house. It's all on loan,
this coast, including my great-aunt's house
that we salvaged all skeletal,
revealing a truth about itself
in lath and plaster I had waited years
to find. Shreds of old wallpaper
spoke in tongues when the wind thrilled them,
dead seascrolls. I find myself

peeling, unsure of my chintz.
They jacked them all out
in the seventies, the marble fireplaces.
What's left is lined up lonely
in salvage yards waiting to be
reclaimed by the home-comers,
incomers and downshifters
in a sawdust mist. Romantic until
you realise the tilt of it.

Bolted Down

This is the land, although you'd not believe it
to look at his lean-to, my grandpa who'd
nail down every piece of wood he owned
in case a north-westerly tipped the ship of the shed
thirty degrees and sent pens and compasses to
the far end wall. Like a priest-hole, hidden by a curtain,
down a corridor at the back of the house,
you'd open a door into his bolt-hole,
a chest of drawers jarring with ship's
carpenter's tools and a worktop where he'd plot
a chart of their garden as it slipped
into the night of the sea. Nothing compared to
the Roaring Forties, of course, during his fifty years
at the helm. Behind that chest a narrow door
led to two interconnecting clapboard rooms,
the walls hung with string and hooks,
hammers and screws, like artwork.

You Can't Get Away From It All

by definition. *Many of us dream of
escaping from it all to live by the sea,*
it says in the brochure. *In 2004 we did
just that.* Trouble is you never can
get away from it all, no matter how far
you run. There is always an edge
to the land that you cannot go beyond,
except by boat for a few hours a day
to avoid talking to your guests, and that's
only when the sea's calm. We're all
faced by the same set of issues
somewhere along the line of land
and life. If it's any consolation,
you will get away from it all
eventually when your house is
washed into the sea.
But that could take a while.
The only place
the brochure authors can escape to
is the attic, having let out
their rooms with views. Which is fine.
If you put the right spin on it.

Attic

We've all been banished to a garret
in our time, mainly by choice
and for a year. After that you begin to

get cabin fever. *Remember when*
we both lived in attics in Paris?
wrote my friend, Mary-Lou, before
leukaemia killed her off at 36
last year. Our connection across the
rooftops of the city lay in
the opening and closing of shutters,
steep tiles, angles and wires which
framed our picture of 'abroad'. For her,
it was the morning heels on cobbles.
For me, it was the cabin bed
in the lee of the chimney breast,
the closest I got to the feel of the sea
all year. You're always nearer to a storm
in an attic, the rattle of a casement window
framing the sea slavering over the pier.

Welsh Knot

The thing is, you have to adapt, move on
my neighbour of five weeks a year tells me.
Adapt to what is not clear, nor who
needs to adapt. So here's an adaptation
from his story: that those in this village
have 'adapted better' to speaking English
than towns up the coast. I suggest
he might like to adapt to learning
the language of the country he's
chosen to buy a house in. Why not
tell him the story of the Welsh Not?

Heard of two letters on wood that hung
around the neck of any child who
dared to speak their mother tongue
at school? The only Welsh knot he's heard of is
the Celtic sticker in his kitchen window.

On A Timer

The light's on but no one's at home.
Down the long winter hours of seaspray
spat at the cottage windows, the unlit
fires and unslept-in beds, the garden
wound up in itself, the clock stuck
at a quarter past one every day
for four months, no hearts ticking
in the twitching net curtains,
at least there's a light in the hall
on a timer. After all,
it's the thought that counts,
isn't it? How long before
a village full of summer
houses enters the winter
of its life? Until
half the cottages crumble
into the sea? It's ticking.
Can you hear it?

Gardens Down To The Sea

'Down' being the operative word.
A garden needs atmosphere, mystery
and suspense said the designer.
Erosion provides you with quite a bit of that
and the heavier the rainfall, the worse
the slippage. A tree
falling into the arms of
another, the whisper of cracks around
the front door. Until ten years ago,
there was a house across the road called
Water's Edge, with fields of bird's foot trefoil
leading down to the sea which now
greets us with its frothy laugh
at the front gate, flinging bits of
chimney and lintel onto
what remains of our lawn.
Storws Wen is the worst.
Built three fields from the sea, now it perches
on a bed of clay just above the waters.
Cracking views, though. Well quite.

Elsinore

There is no other way
than to shape this wake in wedding-rig

and colour in the driftwood bits that chase us veiled
across the Channel in aquatic ink,

drawing out a paragon of tinderlight
fascicules with which to write the tale.

Oh and how crisp his shirt hanging white
in the cabin on the mess deck, frothing

at the cuff. How toptail to stern his shoes
and gilded brocade on the sleeve as dreamed

as the folded handkerchief proud
on the bowsprit I myself tied like a promise

last week. The latitude clues consisted merely of
a glove falling out of a wardrobe like a loose

hand and made me think of a night
in Hatcase Lane when, tall as a sequoia

he stood, red-musketed, voice rough as
rope, uncaulked. All that remains are his

cream breeches, lifeless on the hammock,
merely a signifier of him, but not his flesh, his

tumble-black hair that makes me scour the ship
for sight of arm or foot, his ruff-dashing

stride across the quarterdeck.
The field of lavender agrees in twilight

purple, delicious as the sky at four a.m.
when I launch my four-oared coble and row

with you, my father, to save the flounderers,
like people at night guided by the phosphorescent

tracks of snails. In wreck-time, where we come from
in Pembrey, they cut the fingers off dead sailors

to keep their rings. O ring, cut finger, so shine,
so toll all the Hurst Castle wave-ache long

or chill the liver in the Yardarm. Collaborate however
they will, the elements cannot unearth

her body. I am the only link my father has
with the corpse of my mother, her portugal

burial, not a hair out of place, even the double
tulip on her coffin, the windows

in the Ward Room slanting diamondly,
bookshelves sliding towards

the mizzen mast below deck,
dining table nailed to the floor, our sails

intimate with the wind.

The Glass Path

I was eight and asleep
when the first bottle
hit the wall,
thrown across
the table below
my room.
She was crying
by the remains
of the fire. *Why
is being drunk
so important to you?*
I still don't have
an answer to that.
When the rope
broke
on the candelabra
on my 40th birthday,
a bottle
of Zinfandel
slivered into
the same table
he'd perched at
for years half-cut.
I was celebrating
the age at which
he'd already
spent half his life

drunk. Picking
the stabbed shards
out, I could see how
he would always be
embedded in it,
this table at which
he'd help me
with long division.
Algebra and alcohol
was an equation
I couldn't
add up
at this staged table
on which I'd posed,
aged six, for a portrait
whose crash
later appalled me
in the hall.
His parents' greenhouse
fell apart
in the first storm
of this year,
a glass jigsaw
all down the garden path
leading to
the lake,
its frozen face

giving nothing away.
In the two days
it took me
to pick the pieces
up, I finally
understood
how much it had cost
him to find his path
again,
feel tomatoes bloom
every year
in that glass room
before
he went through
the windscreen.

Doing Time

And so it happened I found myself
for the first time in two years
propping up the bar of the Three Tuns
in Borehamwood, not really
my local, only *I'd not got*
much choice, I was thinking
as I pulled out the only five-pound note
I'd seen all year, uncurling it
on oak like a revelation when
some bloke tapped my elbow
as they would in the days before
I changed my clothes
to white sheets, black shoes.
So where're you from, love?

I presumed the startled look meant
he knew the place, so as he choked
on his third Guinness I recounted
how, barely an hour ago, I had
unveiled and crept below
the level of the hedge to avoid
setting off the lights, thereby
alerting the nuns who would
otherwise have had to summon
a committee to determine whether
permission should be granted
or not on this occasion; and why
I felt the need to leave the grounds
at all. *Why indeed*, I thought, as I

tiptoed back to aforesaid hedge
in the only pair of heels

I'd kept. Exactly when
they took against me was
hard to say as I'd scrubbed
enough floors in my time and
cooked a hundred pies, picked up
all the leaves in autumn, one
by one, visited the elderly, sick
and dying, led vespers, sang and read.
The thought I might be,
well, *writing a book* was
a little troubling.

So when I tried to apply
to travel the two hundred and
sixty miles to spend one day
with my mother who was
dying in the hills, the Superior said
she must be *really* ill for you
to even think of asking.
When they finally voted me
out, in my own time, of course,
but preferably before the 4th,
I could think of only one reply
as to 'whether I'd be able
to re-adjust without help':
not in these shoes.

Snowstorm

She is looking into his eyes
as the flakes fall, her left leg poised
to skate. If I could see her face
I know it would be more intense

than the deep green backdrop of pines
in mandatory rows behind her.
He holds her hands together,
tight, like someone making a pledge.

Not that she needs to be propped up
in that stiff skirt. Unsuitably
dressed or not, what does it matter?

They're both drowning in this bell jar.
If I shake it again, their glittery
still encounter whirls submerged.